Positive thinking has been scientifically
proven to improve your work life,
physical and mental health,
and relationships. Reading, reciting, and
speaking quotes and affirmations helps
to manifest your desires, dreams, and
goals.

Table of Mind Food :

Dishes On:

- Positivity

- Inspiration

- GET UP AND DO IT

- Motivation

- SUCCESS

- Spiritual

- Goals

- Change

- AFFIRMATIONS

- ATTITUDE

IF YOU
NEVER KNOW
FAILURE
YOU WILL
NEVER KNOW
SUCCESS
-Sugar Ray Leonard
@JAB_BOX

Motivational quotes **affect our brain, our behavior, and our lives** because they make us feel like we are in control of our own success, that we have **self-efficacy.** Quotes make us believe that we have the confidence to complete a task successfully, which is different than having the motivation to succeed.

POSITIVE DISH

1. "A vision without activity will never materialize"-Clint From Flint (TNV)

This was a quote I created in 2004 after getting into network marketing and reading my first personal development book.

My take: It exemplifies what I was learning at the time and looking to learn. You must see the goal every day. Not just see it but work towards the goal every day!

2. "Extraordinary things are always hiding in places people never think to look." —Jodi Picoul

3. "Setting goals is the first step in turning the invisible into the visible." —Tony Robbins

4. "You can have it all. Just not all at once." —Oprah Winfrey

5. "I've missed more than 9000 shots in my career I've lost almost 300 games. 26 times I've been trusted to take the game winning shot and missed. I've failed over and over and over again in my life. And that is why I succeed." —Michael Jordan

6. "Say something positive and you'll see something positive." —Jim Thompson

7. "All you need is the plan, the road map, and the courage to press on to your destination." —Earl Nightingale

8. "Train your mind to see the good in every situation." —Unknown

9. "If you can stay positive in a negative situation, you win." —Unknown

10. "Stay positive. Better days are on their way." —Unknown

11. "Only in the darkness can you see the stars." —Martin Luther King, Jr.

12. "I dwell in possibility." —Emily Dickinson

13. "A goal is not always meant to be reached, it often serves simply as something to aim at." – Bruce Lee

14. "A No. 2 pencil and a dream can take you anywhere." —Joyce Meyer

15. "In a gentle way, you can shake the world." —Mahatma Gandhi

16. "Be yourself and people will like you."
—Jeff Kinney

17. "Each day provides its own gifts." —
Marcus Aurelius

18. "Happiness is a butterfly, which when
pursued, is always just beyond your
grasp, but which, if you will sit down
quietly, may alight upon you." —
Nathaniel Hawthorne

19. "You do not find the happy life. You
make it." —Thomas S. Monson

20. "Inspiration comes from within
yourself. One has to be positive. When
you're positive, good things happen." —
Deep Roy

21. "Those who don't believe in magic will
never find it." —Roald Dahl

22. "Sometimes you will never know the
value of a moment, until it becomes a
memory." —Dr. Seuss

23. "The most wasted of days is one without laughter." —E. E. Cummings

24. "To win big, you sometimes have to take big risks." —Bill Gates

25. "To live a fulfilled life, we need to keep creating the 'what is next', of our lives. Without dreams and goals there is no living, only merely existing, and that is not why we are here." —Mark Twain

26. "Try to be a rainbow in someone's cloud." —Maya Angelou

27. "What lies behind you and what lies in front of you, pales in comparison to what lies inside of you." —Ralph Waldo Emerson

28. "The moment where you doubt you can fly, you cease for ever being able to do it." —Peter Pan J.M. Barrie

29. "Think and wonder. Wonder and think." —Dr. Suess

30. "Just for the record darling, not all positive change feels positive in the beginning." —S. C. Lourie

31. "Thousands of candles can be lighted from a single candle, and the life of the candle will not be shortened. Happiness never decreases by being shared." — Buddha

32. "As we express our gratitude, we must never forget that the highest appreciation is not to utter words, but to live by them." —John F. Kennedy

33. "No act of kindness, no matter how small, is ever wasted." —Aesop

34. "Most people are nice when you finally see them." —Harper Lee

35. "When you are imagining, you might as well imagine something worth while." —Lucy Maud Montgomery

36. "What we think, we become." — Buddha

37. "No matter what people tell you, words and ideas can change the world." — Robin Williams

38. "Whoever is happy will make others happy too." —Anne Frank

39. "Memories of our lives, of our works and our deeds will continue in others." — Rosa Parks

40. "All our dreams can come true, if we have the courage to pursue them." —Walt Disney

41. "Twenty years from now you will be more disappointed by the things that you didn't do than by the ones you did do." — H.Jackson Brown Jr

42. "Salvation lies within." —Warden Samuel Norton

43. "Jump in with both feet and be brave." —Sujit Choudhry

44. "If I got rid of my demons, I'd lose my angels." —Tennessee Williams

45. "Always let your conscience be your guide." —Jiminy Cricket

46. "Do what is true to your soul." —Malini Saba

47. "I want to reach my potential, impact my world, and leave a legacy." —Seth Buechley

48. "Today is a good day to try." —Quasimodo, *The Hunchback of Notre Dame*

49. "Make your life matter and have fun doing it." —Aaron Hurst

50. "Choose to be optimistic, it feels better." —Dalai Lama

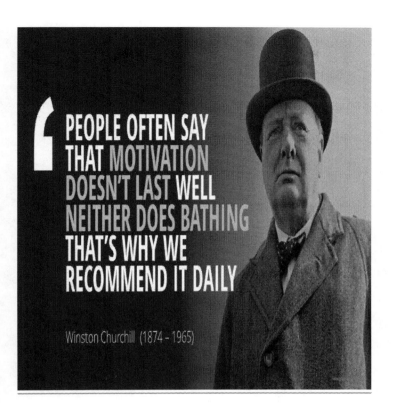

PEOPLE OFTEN SAY
THAT MOTIVATION
DOESN'T LAST WELL
NEITHER DOES BATHING
THAT'S WHY WE
RECOMMEND IT DAILY

Winston Churchill (1874 - 1965)

51. "Surround yourself with positive people." —Rod Rohrich

52. "We have to collectively work together to improve the world." —Samuel Strauch

53. "Base your relationships on the right values." —Dick Gephardt

54. "Be the change that you wish to see in the world." —Mahatma Gandhi

55. "The joy of life is becoming a person you are proud of." —Bill Orender

56. "The truly rich are those who enjoy what they have." —Yiddish Proverb

57. "My friends, love is better than anger. Hope is better than fear. Optimism is better than despair. So let us be loving, hopeful and optimistic. And we'll change the world." —Jack Layton

58. "Let your life lightly dance on the edges of time like dew on the tip of a leaf." —Rabindranath Tagore

59. "When you realize how precious and fragile life is, it changes your whole perspective." —Ryan O'Donnell

60. "The next choice is the most important choice." —George Wells

61. "A friend may be waiting behind a stranger's face."—Maya Angelou

62. "When the sun is shining I can do anything; no mountain is too high, no trouble too difficult to overcome." —Wilma Rudolph

63. "We may not have hit the peak yet, but we are on the journey up." —Brian Nhira

64. "The power of imagination makes us infinite." —John Muir

65. "Do good and good will come to you."
—Adam Lowy

66. "Make a determination that you will live your purpose today." —Daniel Budzinski

67. "Recognize what you have inside you."
—Eric Pulier

68. "The world is full of magical things patiently waiting for our wits to grow sharper." —Bertrand Russell

69. "Words can inspire, thoughts can provoke, but only action truly brings you closer to your dreams." —Brad Sugars

70. "May your troubles be less and your blessings be more." —Irish Blessing

71. "Few things can help an individual more than to place responsibility on him, and to let him know that you trust him." –Booker T. Washington

72. "Look at the sparrows; they do not know what they will do in the next moment. Let us literally live from moment to moment."—Mahatma Gandhi

73. "When I let go of what I am, I become what I might be." —Lao Tzu

74. "The mind is everything. What you think you become." —Buddha

75. "Some men see things as they are and say why—I dream things that never were and say why not." —George Bernard Shaw

INSPIRATIONAL DISH

It is impossible to stop a man or woman who will not quit- Mike Humes (TNV)

My millionaire mentor , Mike Humes, has been saying this for over 20+ years. I take this to mean , You only fail when you quit!

1. "When you have a dream, you've got to grab it and never let go."
— Carol Burnett

2. "Nothing is impossible. The word itself says 'I'm possible!'"
— Audrey Hepburn

3. "There is nothing impossible to they who will try."
— Alexander the Great

4. "The bad news is time flies. The good news is you're the pilot."
— Michael Altshuler

5. "Life has got all those twists and turns. You've got to hold on tight and off you go."
— Nicole Kidman

6. "Keep your face always toward the sunshine, and shadows will fall behind you."
— Walt Whitman

7. "Be courageous. Challenge orthodoxy. Stand up for what you believe in. When you are in your rocking chair talking to your grandchildren many years from now, be sure you have a good story to tell."
— Amal Clooney

8. "You make a choice: continue living your life feeling muddled in this abyss of self-misunderstanding, or you find your identity independent of it. You draw your own box."
— Duchess Meghan

9. "I just want you to know that if you are out there and you are being really hard on yourself right now for something that has happened ... it's normal. That is what is going to happen to you in life. No one gets through unscathed. We are all going to have a few scratches on us. Please be kind to yourselves and stand up for yourself, please."
— Taylor Swift

10. "Success is not final, failure is not fatal: it is the courage to continue that counts."
- Winston Churchill

11. "You define your own life. Don't let other people write your script."
— Oprah Winfrey

12. "You are never too old to set another goal or to dream a new dream."
— Malala Yousafzai

13. "At the end of the day, whether or not those people are comfortable with how you're living your life doesn't matter. What matters is whether you're comfortable with it."
— Dr. Phil

14. "People tell you the world looks a certain way. Parents tell you how to think. Schools tell you how to think. TV. Religion. And then at a certain point, if you're lucky, you realize you can make up your own mind. Nobody sets the rules but you. You can design your own life."
— Carrie Ann Moss

15. "For me, becoming isn't about arriving somewhere or achieving a certain aim. I see it instead as forward motion, a means

of evolving, a way to reach continuously toward a better self. The journey doesn't end."
— Michelle Obama

16. "Spread love everywhere you go."
— Mother Teresa

17. "Do not allow people to dim your shine because they are blinded. Tell them to put some sunglasses on."
— Lady Gaga

18. "If you make your internal life a priority, then everything else you need on the outside will be given to you and it will be extremely clear what the next step is."
— Gabrielle Bernstein

19. "You don't always need a plan. Sometimes you just need to breathe, trust, let go and see what happens."
— Mandy Hale

20. "You can be everything. You can be the infinite amount of things that people are."
— Kesha

21. "What lies behind you and what lies in front of you, pales in comparison to what lies inside of you."
— Ralph Waldo Emerson

22. "I want to be in the arena. I want to be brave with my life. And when we make the choice to dare greatly, we sign up to get our asses kicked. We can choose courage or we can choose comfort, but we can't have both. Not at thsame time."
— Brene Brown

23. "I'm going to be gone one day, and I have to accept that tomorrow isn't promised. Am I OK with how I'm living today? It's the only thing I can help. If I didn't have another one, what have I done with all my todays? Am I doing a good job?"
— Hayley Williams

24. "I am experienced enough to do this. I am knowledgeable enough to do this. I am prepared enough to do this. I am mature enough to do this. I am brave enough to do this."
— Alexandria Ocasio-Cortez

25. "Belief creates the actual fact."
— William James

26. "No matter what people tell you, words and ideas can change the world."
— Robin Williams as John Keating

27. "I'm not going to continue knocking that old door that doesn't open for me. I'm going to create my own door and walk through that."
— Ava DuVernay

28. "It is during our darkest moments that we must focus to see the light."
— Aristotle

29. "Not having the best situation, but seeing the best in your situation is the key to happiness."
— Marie Forleo

30. "Believe you can and you're halfway there."
- Theodore Roosevelt

31. "Weaknesses are just strengths in the wrong environment."
— Marianne Cantwell

32. "Just don't give up trying to do what you really want to do. Where there is love and inspiration, I don't think you can go wrong."
— Ella Fitzgerald

33. "Silence is the last thing the world will ever hear from me."
— Marlee Matlin

34. "In a gentle way, you can shake the world."
— Mahatma Gandhi

35. "Learning how to be still, to really be still and let life happen—that stillness becomes a radiance."
— Morgan Freeman

36. "Everyone has inside of him a piece of good news. The good news is that you don't know how great you can be! How much you can love! What you can accomplish! And what your potential is!"
— Anne Frank

37. "All you need is the plan, the road map, and the courage to press on to your destination."
— Earl Nightingale

38. "I care about decency and humanity and kindness. Kindness today is an act of rebellion."
— Pink

39. "If you have good thoughts they will shine out of your face like sunbeams, and

you will always look lovely."
— Roald Dahl

40. "Try to be a rainbow in someone's cloud."
— Maya Angelou

Unsplash

41. "We must let go of the life we have planned, so as to accept the one that is waiting for us."
— Joseph Campbell

42. "Find out who you are and be that person. That's what your soul was put on this earth to be. Find that truth, live that truth, and everything else will come."
— Ellen DeGeneres

43. "Real change, enduring change, happens one step at a time."
— Ruth Bader Ginsburg

44. "Wake up determined, go to bed satisfied."
— Dwayne "The Rock" Johnson

45. "Nobody built like you, you design yourself."
— Jay-Z

46. "You gain strength, courage, and confidence by every experience in which you really stop to look fear in the face. You are able to say to yourself, 'I lived through this horror. I can take the next thing that comes along.' You must do the thing you think you cannot do."
— Eleanor Roosevelt

47. "I tell myself, 'You've been through so much, you've endured so much, time will allow me to heal, and soon this will be just another memory that made me the strong woman, athlete, and mother I am today.'"
— Serena Williams

48. "Live your beliefs and you can turn the world around."
— Henry David Thoreau

49. "Our lives are stories in which we write, direct and star in the leading role. Some chapters are happy while others bring lessons to learn, but we always have the power to be the heroes of our own adventures."
— Joelle Speranza

50. "Life is like riding a bicycle. To keep your balance, you must keep moving."
- Albert Einstein

51. "Don't try to lessen yourself for the world; let the world catch up to you."
— Beyoncé

52. "There's nothing more powerful than not giving a f—k."
— Amy Schumer

53. "Faith is love taking the form of aspiration."
—William Ellery Channing

54. "When it comes to luck, you make your own."
— Bruce Springsteen

55. "If you don't like the road you're walking, start paving another one!"
— Dolly Parton

56. "I have learned over the years that when one's mind is made up, this diminishes fear; knowing what must be done does away with fear."
— Rosa Parks

57. "The moral of my story is the sun always comes out after the storm. Being optimistic and surrounding yourself with positive loving people is for me, living life on the sunny side of the street."
— Janice Dean

58. "We generate fears while we sit. We overcome them by action."
— Dr. Henry Link

59. "Dreams don't have to just be dreams. You can make it a reality; if you just keep pushing and keep trying, then eventually you'll reach your goal. And if that takes a few years, then that's great, but if it takes 10 or 20, then that's part of the process."
— Naomi Osaka

60."We are not our best intentions. We are what we do."
— Amy Dickinson

61. "I've noticed when I fear something, if I just end up doing it, I'm grateful in the end."
— Colleen Hoover

62. "Work hard, know your s—t, show your s—t, and then feel entitled."
— Mindy Kaling

63. "We've been making our own opportunities, and as you prove your worth and value to people, they can't put you in a box. You hustle it into happening, right?"
— Jennifer Lopez

64. "When you've seen beyond yourself, then you may find, peace of mind is waiting there."
— George Harrison

65. "Out of the mountain of despair, a stone of hope."
— Martin Luther King, Jr.

66. "What you get by achieving your goals is not as important as what you become by achieving your goals."
- Zig Ziglar

67. "I'm realizing how much I've diminished my own power. I'm not doing that no more."
— Alicia Keys

68. "You are never too old to set another goal or to dream a new dream."
— C.S. Lewis

69. "I believe that if you'll just stand up and go, life will open up for you. Something just motivates you to keep moving."
— Tina Turner

70. "How wild it was, to let it be."
— Cheryl Strayed

71. "The simple act of listening to someone and making them feel as if they have truly been heard is a most treasured gift."
— L. A. Villafane

72. "You have to be where you are to get where you need to go."
— Amy Poehler

73. "Don't be afraid. Because you're going to be afraid. But remember when you become afraid, just don't be afraid."
— Joan Jett

74. "We need to take risks. We need to go broke. We need to prove them wrong, simply by not giving up."
— Awkwafina

75. "The only limit to our realization of tomorrow will be our doubts today."
— Franklin Delano Roosevelt

GET UP AND DO IT DISH

BUT NOT For the Rebel Things would not have changed- Esther Stanley

My take: "It takes those people, who do not follow the current model, to expose the possibilities of change."

1. Life is about making an impact, not making an income. --Kevin Kruse

2. Whatever the mind of man can conceive and believe, it can achieve. --Napoleon Hill

3. Strive not to be a success, but rather to be of value. --Albert Einstein

4. Two roads diverged in a wood, and I—I took the one less traveled by, And that has made all the difference. --Robert Frost

5. I attribute my success to this: I never gave or took any excuse. --Florence Nightingale

6. You miss 100% of the shots you don't take. --Wayne Gretzky

8. The most difficult thing is the decision to act, the rest is merely tenacity. --Amelia Earhart

9. Every strike brings me closer to the next home run. –Babe Ruth

10. Definiteness of purpose is the starting point of all achievement. –W. Clement Stone

11. Life isn't about getting and having, it's about giving and being. –Kevin Kruse

12. Life is what happens to you while you're busy making other plans. –John Lennon

13. We become what we think about. – Earl Nightingale

14.Twenty years from now you will be more disappointed by the things that you didn't do than by the ones you did do, so throw off the bowlines, sail away from safe harbor, catch the trade winds in your sails. Explore, Dream, Discover. –Mark Twain

15. Life is 10% what happens to me and 90% of how I react to it. –Charles Swindoll

16. The most common way people give up their power is by thinking they don't have any. –Alice Walker

17. The mind is everything. What you think you become. –Buddha

18. The best time to plant a tree was 20 years ago. The second best time is now. –Chinese Proverb

19. An unexamined life is not worth living. –Socrates

20. Eighty percent of success is showing up. –Woody Allen

21. Your time is limited, so don't waste it living someone else's life. –Steve Jobs

22. Winning isn't everything, but wanting to win is. –Vince Lombardi

23. I am not a product of my circumstances. I am a product of my decisions. –Stephen Covey

24. Every child is an artist. The problem is how to remain an artist once he grows up. –Pablo Picasso

25. You can never cross the ocean until you have the courage to lose sight of the shore. –Christopher Columbus

26. I've learned that people will forget what you said, people will forget what you did, but people will never forget how you made them feel. –Maya Angelou

27. Either you run the day, or the day runs you. –Jim Rohn

28. Whether you think you can or you think you can't, you're right. –Henry Ford

29. The two most important days in your life are the day you are born and the day you find out why. –Mark Twain

30. Whatever you can do, or dream you can, begin it. Boldness has genius, power and magic in it. –Johann Wolfgang von Goethe

31. The best revenge is massive success.
−Frank Sinatra

32. People often say that motivation doesn't last. Well, neither does bathing. That's why we recommend it daily. −Zig Ziglar

33. Life shrinks or expands in proportion to one's courage. −Anais Nin

34. If you hear a voice within you say "you cannot paint," then by all means paint and that voice will be silenced. −Vincent Van Gogh

35. There is only one way to avoid criticism: do nothing, say nothing, and be nothing. −Aristotle

36. Ask and it will be given to you; search, and you will find; knock and the door will be opened for you. −Jesus

37. The only person you are destined to become is the person you decide to be. −Ralph Waldo Emerson

38. Go confidently in the direction of your dreams. Live the life you have imagined. –Henry David Thoreau

39. When I stand before God at the end of my life, I would hope that I would not have a single bit of talent left and could say, I used everything you gave me. – Erma Bombeck

40. Few things can help an individual more than to place responsibility on him, and to let him know that you trust him. –Booker T. Washington

41. Certain things catch your eye, but pursue only those that capture the heart. – Ancient Indian Proverb

42. Believe you can and you're halfway there. –Theodore Roosevelt

43. Everything you've ever wanted is on the other side of fear. –George Addair

44. We can easily forgive a child who is afraid of the dark; the real tragedy of life is when men are afraid of the light. – Plato

45. Teach thy tongue to say, "I do not know," and thou shalt progress. – Maimonides

46. Start where you are. Use what you have. Do what you can. –Arthur Ashe

47. When I was 5 years old, my mother always told me that happiness was the key to life. When I went to school, they asked me what I wanted to be when I grew up. I wrote down 'happy'. They told me I didn't understand the assignment, and I told them they didn't understand life. —John Lennon

48. Fall seven times and stand up eight. —Japanese Proverb

49. When one door of happiness closes, another opens, but often we look so long at the closed door that we do not see the one that has been opened for us. —Helen Keller

50. Everything has beauty, but not everyone can see. —Confucius

51. How wonderful it is that nobody need wait a single moment before starting to improve the world. —Anne Frank

52. When I let go of what I am, I become what I might be. —Lao Tzu

53. Life is not measured by the number of breaths we take, but by the moments that take our breath away. –Maya Angelou

54. Happiness is not something readymade. It comes from your own actions. –Dalai Lama

55. If you're offered a seat on a rocket ship, don't ask what seat! Just get on. – Sheryl Sandberg

56. First, have a definite, clear practical ideal; a goal, an objective. Second, have the necessary means to achieve your ends; wisdom, money, materials, and methods. Third, adjust all your means to that end. –Aristotle

57. If the wind will not serve, take to the oars. –Latin Proverb

58. You can't fall if you don't climb. But there's no joy in living your whole life on the ground. –Unknown

59. We must believe that we are gifted for something, and that this thing, at

whatever cost, must be attained. –Marie Curie

60. Too many of us are not living our dreams because we are living our fears. –Les Brown

61. Challenges are what make life interesting and overcoming them is what makes life meaningful. –Joshua J. Marine

62. If you want to lift yourself up, lift up someone else. –Booker T. Washington

63. I have been impressed with the urgency of doing. Knowing is not enough; we must apply. Being willing is not enough; we must do. –Leonardo da Vinci

64. Limitations live only in our minds. But if we use our imaginations, our possibilities become limitless. – Jamie Paolinetti

65. You take your life in your own hands, and what happens? A terrible thing, no one to blame. –Erica Jong

66. What's money? A man is a success if he gets up in the morning and goes to bed at night and in between does what he wants to do. –Bob Dylan

67. I didn't fail the test. I just found 100 ways to do it wrong. –Benjamin Franklin

68. In order to succeed, your desire for success should be greater than your fear of failure. –Bill Cosby

69. A person who never made a mistake never tried anything new. – Albert Einstein

70. The person who says it cannot be done should not interrupt the person who is doing it. –Chinese Proverb

71. There are no traffic jams along the extra mile. –Roger Staubach

72. It is never too late to be what you might have been. –George Eliot

73. You become what you believe. – Oprah Winfrey

74. I would rather die of passion than of boredom. –Vincent van Gogh

75. A truly rich man is one whose children run into his arms when his hands are empty. –Unknown

MOTIVATIONAL DISH

There are no losses. There are only lessons

JR Riddle(TNV Mentor)

My take: It's all about perspective and how you look at a thing

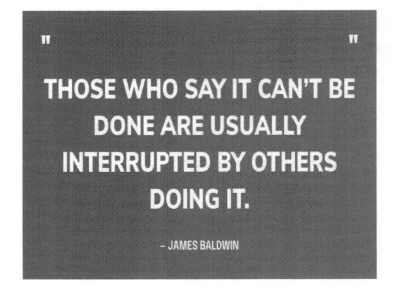

1. "You only have to be right once." — Drew Houston, founder of Dropbox

2. "I'm not afraid to take a swing and miss." — Fred Smith, founder of FedEx Corporation

3. "When there is no struggle, there is no strength." — Oprah Winfrey, media executive

4. "Opportunities don't happen, you create them." — Chris Grosser, entrepreneur

"Nothing will work unless you do." — Maya Angelou, poet

5. "If you love what you do and are willing to do what it takes, it's within your reach." — Steve Wozniak, co-founder of Apple Computer

6. "Setting goals is the first step in turning the invisible into the visible." — Tony Robbins, life coach

7. "There are a ton of great ideas, what is missing is one of yours"- Clint From Flint

8. "Never, never, never give up." — Winston Churchill, former British Prime Minister

9. "Whether you think you can, or you think you can't — You're right." — Henry Ford, founder of Ford Motor Company

10. "Things do not happen. Things are made to happen." — John F. Kennedy, former President of the United States

11. "If you want to achieve greatness stop asking for permission." — Anonymous

12. "I have not failed. I've just found 10,000 ways that won't work." — Thomas A. Edison, inventor

13. "The function of leadership is to produce more leaders, not more followers." — Ralph Nader, political activist

14. "I find that the harder I work, the more luck I seem to have." —Thomas Jefferson, former President of the United States

15. "Don't be afraid to give up the good to go for the great." — John D. Rockefeller, business magnate

18. "Our greatest weakness lies in giving up. The most certain way

to succeed is always to try one

more time." — Thomas A. Edison

19.   "There are no shortcuts to

anywhere worth going." — Beverly

Sills, opera singer

20.   "It's not whether you get

knocked down, it's whether you get

back up." – Vince Lombardi,

Football Hall of Fame coach

21.   "The way to get started is to

quit talking and begin doing." –

Walt Disney, film producer

22.   "If you can't fly, then run. If

you can't run, then walk. If you

can't walk, then crawl, but whatever you do, you have to keep moving forward." – Martin Luther King, Jr., civil rights activist

23.   "You miss 100 percent of the shots you don't take." — Wayne Gretzky, NFL Hall of Famer

24.   "The biggest risk is not taking any risk... In a world that's changing really quickly, the only strategy that is guaranteed to fail is not taking risks." — Mark Zuckerberg, co-founder of Facebook

25. "Preparation is the key to success." — Alexander Graham Bell, co-founder of AT&T

26. "Today a reader. Tomorrow a leader." — Anonymous

27. "Many of life's failures are people who did not realize how close they were to success when they gave up." – Thomas A. Edison

If you change the way you look at things, the things you look at change.

Wayne Dyer

BrainyQuote

28.   "Even if people are still very young, they shouldn't be prevented from saying what they think." — Anne Frank, diarist

29.   "You can, you should, and if you're brave enough to start, you will." – Stephen King, writer

30.   "When you have a dream, you've got to grab it and never let go." — Carol Burnett, actress

Need some extra motivation for your Monday? Use the following quotes for the boost you need to start your week right.

31. "Our greatest glory is not in never falling but in rising every time we fall." — Confucius, Chinese philosopher

32. "The future depends on what you do today." — Mahatma Gandhi, pacifist

33. "If you don't have any shadows you're not in the light." Lady Gaga, singer

34. "It isn't where you came from. It's where you're going that counts." — Ella Fitzgerald, jazz singer

35.   "A ship is always safe at the shore, but that is not what it is built for." — Albert Einstein, theoretical physicist

36.   "Don't wait for the perfect conditions for success to happen; just go ahead and do something." — Dan Miller, writer

37.   "What seems to us as bitter trials are often blessings in disguise." — Oscar Wilde, Irish poet

38.   "Go as far as you can see; when you get there, you'll be able

to see further." Thomas Carlyle, Scottish historian

39.   "You learn more from failure than from success. Don't let it stop you. Failure builds character." — Anonymous

40.   "A river cuts through rock, not because of its power but because of its persistence." — Jim Watkins, American journalist

41.   "Be so good they can't ignore you." — Steve Martin, actor

42.   "Success doesn't come to you, you go to it." Marva Collins, American educator

43.   "With the new day comes new strength and new thoughts." — Eleanor Roosevelt, former First Lady of the United States

44.   "It is never too late to be what you might have been." — George Eliot, novelist

45.   "If I cannot do great things, I can do small things in a great way." — Martin Luther King Jr.

46.   "It's a good day to have a good day." — Anonymous

47.   You didn't come this far to only come this far." — Anonymous

48.   "Work hard in silence, let your success be your noise." — Frank Ocean, singer-songwriter

49.   " A goal should scare you a little, and excite you a lot." Joe Vitale, spiritual teacher

50.   "Don't let yesterday take up too much of today." — Will Rogers, actor

51. "Every morning starts a new page in your story. Make it a great one today." — Doe Zantamata, author

52. "Don't let life discourage you; everyone who got where he is had to begin where he was." — Richard L. Evans, writer

53. "Go the extra mile, it's never crowded."— Anonymous

54. "Keep your sunny side up, keep yourself beautiful, and indulge yourself." — Betsey Johnson, fashion designer

55. "Life is 10% what happens to you and 90% how you react to it." — Charles R. Swindoll, pastor

56. "Life is like riding a bicycle. To keep your balance, you must keep moving." — Albert Einstein

57. "Limit your 'always' and your 'nevers.'" — Amy Poehler, comedian

58. "Nothing is impossible. The word itself says 'I'm possible!'" — Audrey Hepburn, actress

"I'M GLAD TODAY DIDNT START WITHOUT ME. . ."

59.   "You are never too old to set another goal or to dream a new dream." — C.S. Lewis, writer

60.   "Don't let the fear of striking out hold you back." — Babe Ruth, professional baseball player

61.   "Believe me, the reward is not so great without the struggle." Wilma Rudolph, track and field athlete

62.   "When you fall, get right back up." — Lindsay Vonn, professional skier

63.   "If you don't love what you do, you won't do it with much conviction or passion." — Mia Hamm, professional soccer player

64.   "If you aren't going all the way, why go at all?" — Joe Namath, Football Hall of Famer

65.   "Obstacles don't have to stop you. If you run into a wall, don't turn around and give up." — Michael Jordan, basketball icon

66.   "Champions keep playing until they get it right." — Billie Jean King, Tennis Hall of Famer

67.   "You have to believe in yourself when no one else does." — Venus Williams, professional tennis player

68.   "Always make a total effort, even when the odds are against you." — Arnold Palmer, golf icon

69.   "If you have everything under control, you're not moving fast enough." — Mario Andretti, champion racing driver

70.   "It isn't the mountains ahead to climb that wear you out; It's the pebble in your shoe." — Muhammad Ali, champion boxer

71.   "Do not wait; the time will never be just right." — George Herbert, poet

72.   "Too many of us are not living our dreams because we are living our fears." — Les Brown, motivational speaker

73.   "If you can dream it, You can do it." — Walt Disney

74.   "The future belongs to those who believe in the beauty of their dreams." — Eleanor Roosevelt

75.   "Start where you are. Use what you have. Do what — Arthur Ashe, professional tennis player

SUCCESS DISH

You can not hit a target you cannot see!

James Kelly (TNV Mentor)

My take: Always have a goal in mind

1. "If you want to achieve greatness stop asking for permission." --*Anonymous*

2. "Things work out best for those who make the best of how things work out." --*John Wooden*

3. "To live a creative life, we must lose our fear of being wrong." --*Anonymous*

4. "If you are not willing to risk the usual you will have to settle for the ordinary." --*Jim Rohn*

5. "Trust because you are willing to accept the risk, not because it's safe or certain." --*Anonymous*

6. "Take up one idea. Make that one idea your life--think of it, dream of it, live on that idea. Let the brain, muscles, nerves, every part of your body, be full of that idea, and just leave every other idea alone. This is the way to success." --*Swami Vivekananda*

7. "All our dreams can come true if we have the courage to pursue them." -- *Walt Disney*

8. "Good things come to people who wait, but better things come to those

who go out and get them." --

Anonymous

9. "If you do what you always did, you will get what you always got." --

Anonymous

10. "Success is walking from failure to failure with no loss of enthusiasm." --

Winston Churchill

11. "Just when the caterpillar thought the world was ending, he turned into a butterfly." --*Proverb*

12. "Successful entrepreneurs are givers and not takers of positive energy." --*Anonymous*

13. "Whenever you see a successful person you only see the public glories, never the private sacrifices to reach them." -- *Vaibhav Shah*

14. "Opportunities don't happen, you create them." --*Chris Grosser*

15. "Try not to become a person of success, but rather try to become a person of value." --*Albert Einstein*

16. "Great minds discuss ideas;

average minds discuss events; small

minds discuss people." --*Eleanor*

Roosevelt

17. "I have not failed. I've just found

10,000 ways that won't work." --

Thomas A. Edison

STARVE YOUR
DISTRACTIONS,
FEED YOUR
FOCUS.

18. "If you don't value your time,

neither will others. Stop giving away

your time and talents--start charging

for it." --*Kim Garst*

19. "A successful man is one who can lay a firm foundation with the bricks others have thrown at him." --*David Brinkley*

20. "No one can make you feel inferior without your consent." --*Eleanor Roosevelt*

21. "The whole secret of a successful life is to find out what is one's destiny to do, and then do it." --*Henry Ford*

22. "If you're going through hell keep going." --*Winston Churchill*

23. "The ones who are crazy enough to think they can change the world, are the ones who do." --*Anonymous*

24. "Don't raise your voice, improve your argument." --*Anonymous*

25. "What seems to us as bitter trials are often blessings in disguise." -- *Oscar Wilde*

26. "The meaning of life is to find your gift. The purpose of life is to give it away." --*Anonymous*

27. "The distance between insanity and genius is measured only by success." --*Bruce Feirstein*

28. "When you stop chasing the wrong things, you give the right things a chance to catch you." --*Lolly Daskal*

29. "I believe that the only courage anybody ever needs is the courage to follow your own dreams." --*Oprah Winfrey*

30. "No masterpiece was ever created by a lazy artist." --*Anonymous*

31. "Happiness is a butterfly, which when pursued, is always beyond your grasp, but which, if you will sit down quietly, may alight upon you." -- *Nathaniel Hawthorne*

32. "If you can't explain it simply, you don't understand it well enough." -- *Albert Einstein*

33. "Blessed are those who can give without remembering and take without forgetting." --*Anonymous*

34. "Do one thing every day that scares you." --*Anonymous*

35. "What's the point of being alive if you don't at least try to do something remarkable." --*Anonymous*

36. "Life is not about finding yourself. Life is about creating yourself." --

Lolly Daskal

37. "Nothing in the world is more common than unsuccessful people with talent." --*Anonymous*

38. "Knowledge is being aware of what you can do. Wisdom is knowing when not to do it." --*Anonymous*

39. "Your problem isn't the problem. Your reaction is the problem." --*Anonymous*

40. "You can do anything, but not everything." --*Anonymous*

41. "Innovation distinguishes between a leader and a follower." --*Steve Jobs*

42. "There are two types of people who will tell you that you cannot make a difference in this world: those who are afraid to try and those who are afraid you will succeed." --*Ray Goforth*

43. "Thinking should become your capital asset, no matter whatever ups and downs you come across in your life." --*A.P.J. Abdul Kalam*

44. "I find that the harder I work, the more luck I seem to have." --*Thomas Jefferson*

45. "The starting point of all achievement is desire." --*Napoleon Hill*

46. "Success is the sum of small efforts, repeated day-in and day-out." --*Robert Collier*

47. "If you want to achieve excellence, you can get there today. As of this second, quit doing less-than-excellent work." --*Thomas J. Watson*

48. "All progress takes place outside the comfort zone." --*Michael John Bobak*

49. "You may only succeed if you desire succeeding; you may only fail if you do not mind failing." --*Philippos*

50. "Courage is resistance to fear, mastery of fear--not absence of fear." --*Mark Twain*

51. "Only put off until tomorrow what you are willing to die having left undone." --*Pablo Picasso*

52. "People often say that motivation doesn't last. Well, neither does bathing--that's why we recommend it daily." --*Zig Ziglar*

53. "We become what we think about most of the time, and that's the strangest secret." -- *Earl Nightingale*

54. "The only place where success comes before work is in the dictionary." -- *Vidal Sassoon*

55. "Too many of us are not living our dreams because we are living our fears." -- *Les Brown*

56. "I find that when you have a real interest in life and a curious life, that sleep is not the most important thing." -- *Martha Stewart*

57. "It's not what you look at that matters, it's what you see." -- *Anonymous*

58. "The road to success and the road to failure are almost exactly the same." -- *Colin R. Davis*

59. "The function of leadership is to produce more leaders, not more followers." -- *Ralph Nader*

60. "Success is liking yourself, liking what you do, and liking how you do it." -- *Maya Angelou*

61. "As we look ahead into the next century, leaders will be those who empower others." --*Bill Gates*

62. "A real entrepreneur is somebody who has no safety net underneath them." --*Henry Kravis*

63. "The first step toward success is taken when you refuse to be a captive of the environment in which you first find yourself." --*Mark Caine*

64. "People who succeed have momentum. The more they succeed, the more they want to succeed, and the more they find a way to succeed. Similarly, when someone is failing, the tendency is to get on a downward spiral that can even become a self-fulfilling prophecy." -- *Tony Robbins*

65. "When I dare to be powerful, to use my strength in the service of my vision, then it becomes less and less important whether I am afraid." -- *Audre Lorde*

66. "Whenever you find yourself on the side of the majority, it is time to pause and reflect." --*Mark Twain*

67. "The successful warrior is the average man, with laser-like focus." --*Bruce Lee*

68. "There is no traffic jam along the extra mile." --*Roger Staubach*

69. "Develop success from failures. Discouragement and failure are two of the surest stepping stones to success." --*Dale Carnegie*

70. "If you don't design your own life plan, chances are you'll fall into someone else's plan. And guess what they have planned for you? Not much." --*Jim Rohn*

71. "If you genuinely want something, don't wait for it--teach yourself to be impatient." --*Gurbaksh Chahal*

72. "Don't let the fear of losing be greater than the excitement of winning." --*Robert Kiyosaki*

73. "If you want to make a permanent change, stop focusing on the size of your problems and start focusing on the size of you!" -- *T. Harv Eker*

75. "Two roads diverged in a wood and I took the one less traveled by, and that made all the difference." -- *Robert Frost*

SPIRITUAL DISH

Nobody can do for you what you refuse to do for yourself-**Alan Myles (Mentor)**

My take: You have take part in your own rescue

:

1. "The most important person you meet in life is your higher self."

2. "The most expensive things are not on you, around you, or above you, but within you."

3. "Your mind is an entire world, your heart is an entire cosmos, and your soul is an entire universe."

4. "Your humanity is a down payment on your divinity."

5. "Light is full of strength. Nature is full of might. The world is full of energy. The universe is full of power."

6. "Nature is a masterpiece of Earth. Earth is a jewel of light. Light is a showpiece of the cosmos. The universe is a magnum opus of love."

7. "The world has one body, the universe has one soul."

8. "It is impossible for light not to get noticed, especially in the dark."

9. "What is true exercises authority over what is false."

10. "Your higher self is in an eternal struggle with the your lower self."

11. "Truth is awake, even when its eyes are shut."

12. "A slave is one who sells his soul to save his life. A master is one who gives his life to save his soul."

13. "The heart is a classroom. The soul is a teacher. The mind is a student. Life is the exam."

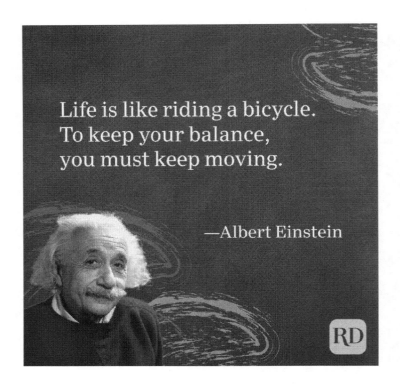

Life is like riding a bicycle.
To keep your balance,
you must keep moving.

—Albert Einstein

14. "The universe is all around you, but its greater dimensions are within you."

15. "The soul is a treasure chest, hidden inside of it are priceless jewels."

16. "The world before your eyes is finite, the universe inside your soul is infinite."

17. "Ignorance reveals our humanity, love announces our divinity."

18. "The world's deepest place is not the ocean, but the human heart."

19. "They wake up with their eyes, you wake up with your soul."

20. "It is light that lets us know we have shadows."

21. "Darkness will always be a servant of light."

22. "Light at the end of the tunnel is inconsequential when your inner light is on."

23. "Medicine heals the body, faith heals the heart, wisdom heals the mind, and love heals the soul."

22. "There is no entrance that joy cannot enter, no door that faith cannot open, no bridge that patience cannot cross, and no wall that love cannot breach."

23. "The world is full of angels; if you can't find one, be one."

24. "To hate is human, to love is divine."

25. "For a beautiful heart, look for the good in others. For a beautiful soul, look for the good in all."

26. "You fall because you are human, and rise because you are divine."

27. "Body is man. Mind is world. Heart is Heaven. Soul is god."

28. "The soul was the first temple, love was the first religion."

29. "Your humanity is a stepping stone to your divinity."

30. "God is the distance between light and darkness."

31. "Truth is the bridge between illusion and reality."

32. "Love is your religion; the whole world is your temple."

33. "If you point to paradise, all the short sighted will see is your finger."

34. "The universe is one body; love is its heartbeat."

35. "Raise your love so high that anger cannot reach it."

36. "Hatred quits when it is tired, love quits when it has won."

37. "The world is a hospital: people are patients, truth is the doctor, and love is the remedy."

38. "The distance between your needs and your wants is contentment."

39. "It is impossible to fill a broken vessel."

40. "Empty pockets teach you a million lessons, full pockets give you a million temptations."

41. "The most valuable things you have money cannot buy."

42. "Generosity is inverted prosperity."

43. "Short prayers with long legs travel far."

44. "Breathe a word of prayer, not anger."

45. "Private prayers are the catalyst for public miracles."

46. "Pebbles that bring you joy are better than diamonds that bring you sorrow."

47. "Truth has clean feet, it leaves no dirt when it sets foot on your soul."

48. "As you light another's path you are lighting your own."

49. "You can curse the dark or you can turn the light on."

50. "Light changes form but never dies."

51. "The universe is a mirror of your soul."

52. "No distance can truly separate you from yourself."

53. "The heart at its weakest can still conquer the mind at its strongest."

54. "The mind is an eternal student of the soul."

55. "Good health is great wealth."

56. "The heart is a wanderer, the mind is its map; love is its destination."

57. "What you seek for others you find for yourself."

58. "Your eyes only see the world, but your soul sees the universe."

59. "Love hopes. Love helps. Love heals. Love hears."

60. "It is easier to tame a thousand bulls than to tame yourself."

61. "Truth does not die because you buried it."

62. "What you sow in the dark you reap in the light."

63. "The eyes are not the widest door to the world, the soul is."

64. "The mind is the ultimate hallway to the world, the soul is the ultimate stairway to the universe."

65. "You are not one in a million, you are one in 7.7 billion."

66. "Light has more space to enter a heart when it is broken."

67. "Love is loud; the soul hears it, even if the universe is deaf."

68. "Wisdom is an ocean whose beginning you can see, but whose end you cannot grasp."

69. "Darkness is fragile; that is why it is always hiding from light."

70. "It is light's beauty that reveals our ugly shadows."

71. "A small light can conquer a great darkness."

72. "When light walks in darkness sprints out."

73. "Where your humanity ends your divinity begins."

74. "Anger is mortal, mercy is divine."

75. "The world says fall in love, but the universe says rise in love."

GOAL DISH

Believe in your heart and soul that you are capable of big things in your life. The only thing that is standing in your way is you.-Chris Polk (PJB)

My take: We already have an appointment with success. It is up to us to show up to the appointment.

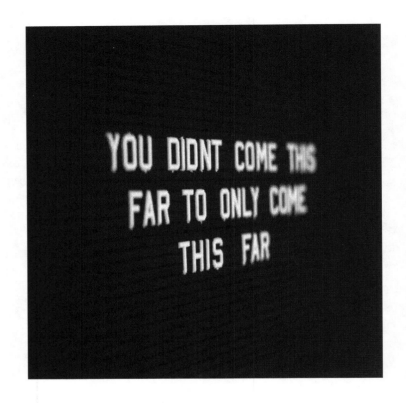

1. "If you want to be happy, set a goal that commands your thoughts, liberates your energy and inspires your hopes." — Andrew Carnegie

2. "Success is the progressive realization of a worthy goal or ideal." —Earl Nightingale

3. "The trouble with not having a goal is that you can spend your life running up and down the field and never score." — Bill Copeland

4. "I think goals should never be easy, they should force you to work, even if they are uncomfortable at the time." —Michael Phelps

5. "You should set goals beyond your reach, so you always have something to live for." —Ted Turner

6. "It must be borne in mind that the tragedy of life doesn't lie in not reaching your goal. The tragedy lies in having no goals to reach." —Benjamin E. Mays

7. "When it is obvious that the goals cannot be reached, don't adjust the goals, adjust the action steps." – Confucius

8. "There's nothing better than achieving your goals, whatever they might be." – Paloma Faith

9. "Stay focused, go after your dreams and keep moving toward your goals." – LL Cool J

10. "You cannot expect to achieve new goals or move beyond your present circumstances unless you change." – Les Brown

11. "Without some goals and some efforts to reach it, no man can live." – John Dewey

12. "Goals are not only necessary to motivate us. They are essential to really keep us alive." – Robert H. Schuller

13. "Set realistic goals, keep re-evaluating, and be consistent." – Venus Williams

14. "Set realistic goals, keep re-evaluating, and be consistent." – Ginni Rometti

15. "It's an up and down thing, the human goals, because the human is always an explorer, an adventurist." – Cesar Millan

16. "If you set your goals ridiculously high and it's a failure, you will fail above everyone else's success." – James Cameron

17. "I am constantly re-evaluating my goals and trying to strike items from my to-do list that aren't critical." – Aisha Tyler

18. "All successful people have a goal. No one can get anywhere unless he knows where he wants to go and what he wants to be or do." – Norman Vincent Peale

19. "Where are the people who don't have goals headed? Those 97 percent end up working for the three percent." – Shiv Khera

20. "I like to tell young people to work hard for your goals and live in the moment." – Nadia Comaneci

21. "People often say I have so much energy, that I never stop; but that's what it takes to accomplish your goals." – Curtis Jackson

22. "My personal goals are to be happy, healthy and to be surrounded by loved ones." – Kiana Tom

23. "You need lofty goals. Then cement it with a great work ethic." – Jerry West

24. "It's harder to stay on top than it is to make the climb. Continue to seek new goals."– Pat Summitt

25. "If you want to live a happy life, tie it to a goal, not to people or things."– Albert Einstein

26. "One way to keep momentum going is to have constantly greater goals."– Michael Korda

27. "If you aim for nothing, you'll hit it every time." – Unknown

28. "The greater danger for most of us isn't that our aim is too high and miss it, but that it is too low and we reach it."– Michelangelo

29. "I am always more interested in what I am about to do than what I have already done."– Rachel Carson

30. "Setting goals is the first step in turning the invisible into the visible."– Tony Robbins

31. "Goals are the fuel in the furnace of achievement."– Brian Tracy

32. "If a goal is worth having, it's worth blocking out the time in your day-to-day life necessary to achieve it."– Jill Koenig

33. "In between goals is a thing called life, that has to be lived and enjoyed."– Sid Caeser

34. "You can always find a solution if you try hard enough."– Lori Greiner

35. "The going is the goal."– Horace Kallen

36. "A good goal is like a strenuous exercise — it makes you stretch."– Mary Kay Ash

37. "Knowing is not enough; we must apply. Willing is not enough; we must do."– Johann Wolfgang von Goethe

38. "There are only two rules for being successful. One, figure out exactly what you want to do, and two, do it."– Mario Cuomo

39. "What you get by achieving your goals is not as important as what you become by achieving your goals."– Henry David Thoreau

40. "Life can be pulled by goals just as surely as it can be pushed by drives." – Viktor Frankl

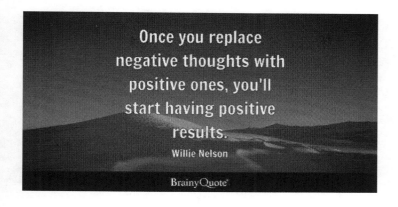

Once you replace
negative thoughts with
positive ones, you'll
start having positive
results.
Willie Nelson

1. "The great glorious masterpiece of man is to know how to live with purpose."– Michel de Montaigne

42. "Intention without action is an insult to those who expect the best from you."– Andy Andrews

43. A goal is not always meant to be reached; it often serves simply as something to aim at." – Bruce Lee

44. "You cannot change your destination overnight, but you can change your direction overnight."– Jim Rohn

45. "If the plan doesn't work, change the plan, but never the goal."– Unknown

46. "Discipline is the bridge between goals and accomplishment."– Jim Rohn

47. "To reach a port, we must sail — Sail, not tie at anchor — Sail, not drift."– Franklin Roosevelt

48. "Be practical as well as generous in your ideals. Keep your eyes on the stars but remember to keep your feet on the ground."– Theodore Roosevelt

49. "The greatest mistake you can make in life is to continually be afraid you will make one."– Elbert Hubbard

50. "Do not let what you cannot do interfere with what you can do."– John Wooden

51. "You are never too old to set a new goal or to dream a new dream." — C.S. Lewis

52. "If we have a goal and a plan, and are willing to take risks and mistakes and work as a team, we can choose to do the hard thing." — Scott Kelly

53. "Never give up. Today is hard, tomorrow will be worse, but the day after tomorrow will be sunshine." - Jack Ma

54. "We think, mistakenly, that success is the result of the amount of time we put in at work, instead of the quality of time we put in." — Arianna Huffington

55. "You can't be that kid standing at the top of the waterslide, overthinking it. You have to go down the chute." - Tina Fey

56. "If something is important enough, even if the odds are against you, you should still do it." - Elon Musk

57. "A goal without a timeline is just a dream." - Robert Herjavec

58. "It always seems impossible until it's done." - Nelson Mandela

59. "Success consists of going from failure to failure without loss of enthusiasm."
- <u>Winston Churchill</u>

60. "You have to be able to get up and dust yourself off and always be going forward." - Rita Moreno

61. "Hustling is putting every minute and all your effort into achieving the goal at hand. Every minute needs to count." - Gary Vaynerchuk

62. "A year from now you may wish you had started today." – Karen Lamb

63. "Dream your own dreams, achieve your own goals. Your journey is your own and unique." – Roy T. Bennett

64. "It's better to be at the bottom of the ladder you want to climb than at the top of the one you don't." –Stephen Kellogg

65. "Life is short, fragile and does not wait for anyone. There will NEVER be a perfect time to pursue your dreams and goals. " – Unknown

66. "A goal is a dream with a deadline." – Napoleon Hill

67. "Things won are done; joy's soul lies in the doing." – William **Shakespeare**

68. "Every ceiling, when reached, becomes a floor, upon which one walks as a matter of course and prescriptive right." – Aldous Huxley

69. "Our goals can only be reached through a vehicle of a plan, in which we must fervently believe, and upon which we must vigorously act. There is no other route to success." – Pablo Picasso

70. "The virtue lies in the struggle, not in the prize." – Richard Monckton Milnes

71. "A good archer is known not by his arrows but by his aim." – Thomas Fuller

72. "In absence of clearly defined goals, we become strangely loyal to performing daily acts of trivia." — Unknown

73. "Think little goals and expect little achievements. Think big goals and win big success." — David Joseph Schwartz

74. "No desired achievement is gained without any goal setting." — Wayne Chirisa

75. "I love the challenge of starting at zero every day and seeing how much I can accomplish."— Martha Stewart

CHANGE DISH

"Anybody can be good, but everyone is not willing to do what it takes to be great! - Anthony Wilson (SMC)

My take: Good is ok but it's average. Being great is next level and requires work. Not many want to put in THAT work.

1. "Change, like <u>healing</u>, takes time." — Veronica Roth

2. "If I am not for myself, who will be for me? But if I am only for myself, what am I? And if not now, when? - Hillel

3. "Things change. And friends leave. Life doesn't stop for anybody." — Stephen Chbosky

4. "Everyone thinks of changing the world, but no one thinks of changing himself." — Leo Tolstoy

5. "Those who cannot change their minds cannot change anything." — George Bernard Shaw

6. "I alone cannot change the world, but I can cast a stone across the waters to create many ripples." — <u>Mother Teresa</u>

7. "Change will not come if we wait for some other person, or if we wait for some other time. We are the ones we've been waiting for. We are the change that we seek." — Barack Obama

8. "The world as we have created it is a process of our thinking. It cannot be changed without changing our thinking." — <u>Albert Einstein</u>

9. "To change one's life: 1. Start immediately. 2. Do it flamboyantly. 3. No exceptions." — William James

10. "Yesterday I was clever, so I wanted to change the world. Today I am wise, so I am changing myself." — Rumi

11. "I don't need a friend who changes when I change and who nods when I nod; my shadow does that much better" - Plutarch

12. "Nothing is so painful to the human mind as a great and sudden change." — Mary Shelley

13. "Life is a series of natural and spontaneous changes. Don't resist them; that only creates sorrow. Let reality be reality. Let things flow naturally forward in whatever way they like." — Lao Tzu

14. "Incredible change happens in your life when you decide to take control of what you do have power over instead of

craving control over what you don't." - Steve Maraboli

15. "I have accepted fear as part of life — specifically the fear of change... I have gone ahead despite the pounding in the heart that says: turn back...." — Erica Jong

16. "We are not trapped or locked up in these bones. No, no. We are free to change. And love changes us. And if we can love one another, we can break open the sky." — Walter Mosley

17. "Change the way you look at things and the things you look at change." — Wayne W. Dyer

18. "Taking a new step, uttering a new word, is what people fear most." — Fyodor Dostoevsky, *Crime and Punishment*

19. "You're always you, and that don't change, and you're always changing, and there's nothing you can do about it." — Neil Gaiman, *The Graveyard Book*

20. "And that is how change happens. One gesture. One person. One moment at a time." — Libba Bray, *The Sweet Far Thing*

21. "Some changes look negative on the surface but you will soon realize that space is being created in your life for something new to emerge." — Eckhart Tolle

22. "Certain things, they should stay the way they are. You ought to be able to stick them in one of those big glass cases and just leave them alone." — J.D. Salinger, *The Catcher in the Rye*

23. "Believe something and the Universe is on its way to being changed. Because you've changed, by believing. Once you've changed, other things start to follow. Isn't that the way it works?" — Diane Duane

24. "Maturity is when you stop complaining and making excuses and start making changes." — Roy T. Bennett

25. "Fashion changes, but style endures." — Coco Chanel

26. "You never change things by fighting the existing reality. To change something, build a new model that makes the existing model obsolete." — Buckminster Fuller

27. "You cannot change what you are, only what you do." — Philip Pullman

28. "Faced with the choice between changing one's mind and proving that there is no need to do so, almost everyone gets busy on the proof. - John Kenneth Galbraith

29. "Time takes it all, whether you want it to or not." — Stephen King, *The Green Mile*

30. "No matter who you are, no matter what you did, no matter where you've come from, you can always change, become a better version of yourself." — Madonna

31. "The philosophers have only interpreted the world, in various ways. The point, however, is to change it." — Karl Marx

32. "I find the best way to love someone is not to change them, but instead, help them reveal the greatest version of themselves." — Steve Maraboli

33. "All that you touch
You Change.
All that you Change
Changes you.
The only lasting truth
is Change.
God is Change." — Octavia E. Butler

STAY CLOSE
TO PEOPLE
WHO FEEL LIKE
SUNSHINE.

34. "Every woman that finally figured out her worth, has picked up her suitcases of pride and boarded a flight to freedom, which landed in the valley of change." — Shannon L. Alder

35. "Anger, resentment and <u>jealousy</u> doesn't change the heart of others-- it only changes yours." — Shannon Alder

36. "If you're in a bad situation, don't worry it'll change. If you're in a good situation, don't worry it'll change." — John A. Simone, Sr.

37. "One child, one teacher, one book, one pen can change the world." — Malala Yousafzai

38. "When people are ready to, they change. They never do it before then, and sometimes they die before they get around to it. You can't make them change if they don't want to, just like when they do want to, you can't stop them." — Andy Warhol

39. "No one can tell what goes on in between the person you were and the person you become. No one can chart that blue and lonely section of hell. There are no maps of the change. You just come out the other side. Or you don't." — Stephen King, *The Stand*

40. "Vulnerability is the birthplace of innovation, creativity and change." — Brene Brown

41. "To improve is to change; to be perfect is to change often." — Winston S. Churchill

42. "Desperation is the raw material of drastic change. Only those who can leave behind everything they have ever believed in can hope to escape." — William S. Burroughs

43. "When you come out of the storm, you won't be the same person who walked in. That's what this storm's all about." — Haruki Murakami

44. "The people who are crazy enough to think they can change the world are the ones who do." — Steve Jobs

45. "I give you this to take with you: Nothing remains as it was. If you know this, you can begin again, with pure joy in the uprooting." — Judith Minty

46. "A bend in the road is not the end of the road... Unless you fail to make the turn." — Helen Keller

47. "Life belongs to the living, and he who lives must be prepared for changes." — Johann Wolfgang von Goethe

48. "Change may not always bring growth, but there is no growth without change." — Roy T. Bennett

49. "True life is lived when tiny changes occur." — Leo Tolstoy

50. "Change begins at the end of your comfort zone." — Roy T. Bennett

51. "Change is the end result of all true learning." — Leo Buscaglia

52. "Our ability to adapt is amazing. Our ability to change isn't quite as spectacular." — Lisa Lutz

53. "Changing is what people do when they have no options left." — Holly Black

54. "To change ourselves effectively, we first had to change our perceptions." — Stephen R. Covey

55. "Nothing is lost . . . Everything is transformed." — Michael Ende

56. "The changes we dread most may contain our salvation." — Barbara Kingsolver

57. "If you want to change attitudes, start with a change in behavior." — Katherine Hepburn

58. "It's not that some people have willpower and some don't... It's that some people are ready to change and others are not." — James Gordon

59. "You tried to change didn't you? Closed your mouth more, tried to be softer, prettier, less volatile, less awake... You can't make homes out of human beings. Someone should have already told you that." — Warsan Shire

60. "Don't knock the weather; nine-tenths of the people couldn't start a conversation if it didn't change once in a while." — Kin Hubbard

61. "Change your thoughts and you change your world." — Norman Vincent Peale

62. "Nothing endures but change." — Heraclitus

63. "The past can teach us, nurture us, but it cannot sustain us. The essence of life is change, and we must move ever forward or the soul will wither and die." — Susanna Kearsley

64. "Anyone who isn't embarrassed of who they were last year probably isn't learning enough." — Alain de Botton

65. "If you want to make enemies, try to change something." - Woodrow Wilson

66. "The only difference between a rut and a grave is their dimensions." - Ellen Glasgow

67. "People are very open-minded about new things, as long as they're exactly like the old ones." - Charles F. Kettering

68. "The great growling engine of change – technology." – Alvin Toffler

69. "Folks, I don't trust children. They're here to replace us." – Stephen Colbert

70. "No matter what people will tell you, words and ideas can change the world." – <u>Robin Williams</u>

71. "People change for two reasons; either they learned a lot or they've been hurt too much." – Unknown

72. "The secret of change is to focus all of your energy, not on fighting the old, but on building the new." – Socrates

73. "Act the way you'd like to be and soon you'll be the way you'd like to act." — Bob Dylan

74. "Change your life today. Don't gamble on the future, act now, without delay." — Simone de Beauvoir

75. "Change is hardest at the beginning, messiest in the middle and best at the end." — Robin Sharma

If you're going to rise, you might as well shine

Affirmations are positive

statements that you repeat to yourself

regularly with the intention of

influencing your subconscious. When

you repeat affirmations, you are

programming your subconscious mind to

focus on positive, empowering thoughts

and beliefs.

1. Money comes to me easily and effortlessly.

2. I constantly attract opportunities that create more money.

3. I am worthy of making more money.

4. I am open and receptive to all the wealth life offers me.

5. My actions create constant prosperity.

6. Money and spirituality can co-exist in harmony.

7. Love & Relationships

8. I am full of positive loving energy.

9. I welcome love and romance into my life.

10. I am in a loving and supportive relationship.

11. I deserve love and I get it in abundance.

12. I am loved, loving and lovable.

13. I am blessed with an incredible family and wonderful friends.

14. I give out love and it is returned to me multiplied manifold.

15. I forgive myself and set myself free.

16.   I believe I can be all that I want to be.

17.   I am in the process of becoming the best version of myself.

18.   I have the freedom & power to create the life I desire.

19.   I choose to be kind to myself and love myself unconditionally.

20.   My possibilities are endless.

21.   I am worthy of my dreams.

22.   I am enough.

23.   I deserve to be healthy and feel good.

24.   Every day I am getting healthier and stronger.

25. I honor my body by trusting the
signals that it sends me.

26. I manifest perfect health by
making smart choices.

27.   29. Being happy comes easy to me.
Happiness is my second nature.

28.   30. Good things are happening.

Our goals should have a deadline! One
of the things that drives and motivates
me daily.!

I will have my $50,000 ring by June 25,
2024, and be the 1st TNV ring earner
from the Great Lake State of Michigan

These Affirmations for black women are courtesy of OURWESTNEST.COM.

I think in abundance, not scarcity.

My black is radiantly beautiful.

My hair texture is beautiful and unique.

I am filled with positive energy and I am evolving with purpose everyday.

Self Care

MORNING AFFIRMATIONS FOR BLACK WOMEN

www.ourwestnest.com

Today is a new day to begin again.

I am committed to all possibilities that lead to a greater purpose.

I attract happiness and joy into my life.

Today I choose me.

Affirmations for Black Women on Self Love

1. Today, I choose me.
2. I know I am smart and capable.
3. I realize I am more than my circumstances.
4. I love the skin I am in.
5. I have the knowledge and ability to achieve everything I want.
6. I will speak positive words and think positive thoughts no matter the situation.
7. I attract success.
8. I know how to make great decisions.
9. My black is radiantly beautiful.
10. My hair texture is beautiful and unique.

Affirmations for Black women on Success

1. I control my success.
2. Today will be a productive day.
3. I will be the best version of myself I can be.
4. I think in abundance, not scarcity.
5. I manifest the great day I want to have.
6. I choose to do great things.
7. Today I will be full of awesome ideas.
8. I will achieve all of my goals for the day.
9. I will be the change I wish to see.
10. Today I will make a positive change by doing something I have never done.

Affirmations for Black Women on Relationships

1. I am a beautiful black woman who deserves love, respect, and kindness.
2. I will show gratitude in all of my relationships.
3. I only have positive thoughts.
4. I respect everyone's journey.
5. I am a loving and caring friend.
6. I appreciate all of my relationships.
7. I will not settle for less than the best from myself or others.
8. I know I can be successful and still root for my peers.
9. I am grateful for every experience.
10. I am worthy to love and be loved, unconditionally.

Affirmations for Black Women on Manifestation

1. Everything I want is everything I should have.
2. I am created by a higher power and I know the woman I am.
3. I attract happiness and joy into my life.
4. I will approach all challenges with gratefulness, confidence, and zest.
5. I will not apologize for being myself.
6. I am comfortable in setting boundaries and sticking with them.
7. I embrace getting out of my comfort zone to explore all the future has to offer.
8. I will make decisions for my happiness.
9. My future is bright.
10. I am manifesting my success all the time

Affirmations for Black Women on confidence

1. I am filled with confidence.
2. I will be open to opportunities.
3. I stay true to myself.
4. I won't let what others say or do get me off track.
5. I am filled with positive energy and evolving with purpose every day.
6. Today I will do something great.
7. Today is a new day to begin again.
8. I am thankful to see another day.
9. I am talented and I belong in this space.
10. I know my value and worthiness

ATTITUDE DISH

Do not complain about what you didn't get from the work you didn't put in! - ICE CUBE

My take: You must put in the work to get the results you want.

1. "If you look the right way, you can see that the whole world is a garden." —Frances Hodgson Burnett

2. "Darkness cannot drive out darkness: only light can do that. Hate cannot drive out hate: only love can do that." —<u>Martin Luther King Jr</u>.

3. "We are all in the gutter, but some of us are looking at the stars." —Oscar Wilde

4. "Live life to the fullest, and focus on the positive." —Matt Cameron

5. "A positive attitude may not solve all our problems but that is the only option we have if we want to get out of problems." —Subodh Gupta

6. "If you don't like something, change it. If you can't change it, change your attitude." —<u>Maya Angelou</u>

7. "Optimism is the faith that leads to achievement; nothing can be done without hope." —Helen Keller

8. "Your attitude can take you forward, or your attitude can take you down. The choice is always yours!" —Catherine Pulsifer

9. "A positive attitude is a person's **passport** to a better tomorrow." —Jeff Keller

10. "Convince yourself every day that you are worthy of a good life. Let go of stress, breathe. Stay positive, all is well." — Germany Kent

11. "Positivity brings about a **peace** of mind which in turn relaxes your whole being." —Suman Arora

12. "Having a positive attitude isn't wishy-washy, it's a concrete and intelligent way to view problems, challenges, and obstacles." —Jeff Moore

13. "The only disability in life is a bad attitude." —Scott Hamilton

14. "A strong positive attitude will create more miracles than any wonder drug." —Patricia Neal

15. "When the negative thoughts come—and they will; they come to all of us—it's not enough to just not dwell on it. ... You've got to replace it with a positive thought." —Joel Osteen

16. "The only disability in life is a bad attitude." —Dale Carnegie

17. "Building a positive attitude begins with having <u>confidence</u> in yourself." — Roger Fritz

18. "Do not allow negative thoughts to enter your mind for they are weeds that strangle confidence." —Bruce Lee

19. "Keep your face always toward the sunshine—and shadows will fall behind you." —Walt Whitman

20. "To be an overachiever you have to be an over-believer." —Dabo Swinney

21. "Life is your seesaw. You may not stay balanced long, but you can aim for a high after every low." —Sanita Belgrave

22. "With a positive attitude it is possible to turn situations of failure into success." —Dan Miller

23. "You're off to great places, today is your day. Your mountain is waiting, so get on your way." —Dr. Seuss

24. "I'm too busy working on my own grass to see if yours is greener." — Unknown

25. "It makes a big difference in your life when you stay positive." —Ellen DeGeneres

26. "Perpetual optimism is a force multiplier." —Colin Powell

27. "The way I see it, if you want the rainbow, you gotta put up with the rain." —Dolly Parton

28. "Nobody can be all smiley all the time, but having a good positive attitude isn't something to shrug off." —Yogi Berra

29. "Never forget to smile because a positive attitude will surely motivate you to get back on your feet after you committed a huge mistake." —Norbert Richards

30. "Nurture your mind with great thoughts, for you will never go any higher than you think." —Benjamin Disraeli

31. "I always like to look on the optimistic side of life, but I am realistic enough to know that life is a complex matter." — Walt Disney

32. "A positive mindset is something every human can work on, and everyone can learn how to enroll in it." —Deeksha Arora

33. "The only time you fail is when you fall down and stay down." —Stephen Richards

34. "To be a great champion you must believe you are the best. If you're not, pretend you are." —Muhammad Ali

35. "With a positive attitude, the world is your oyster. Without it, your world will be filled with ill fate and unfortunate circumstances." —Lorena Laughlin

36. "If you have a positive attitude and constantly strive to give your best effort, eventually you will overcome your immediate problems and find you are ready for greater challenges." —Pat Riley

37. "The greatest discovery of all the time is that a person can change his future by merely changing his attitude." —Marie Osmond

38. "We can complain because rose bushes have thorns or rejoice because thorns have roses." —Unknown

39. "Accept hardship as a necessary discipline." —Lailah Gifty Akita

40. "Faith is having a positive attitude about what you can do and not worrying at all about what you can't do." —Joyce Meyer

41. "It's a little magic trick you can play on yourself. Whenever you feel sad and lonely, just smile and close your eyes. Do it as many times as you have to." —Genki Kawamura

42. "Keep a positive attitude, even if results don't seem to be occurring as quickly as you want them to." —James Thompson

43. "If you can change your mind, you can change your life." —William James

44. "Being what most people think is realistic is only a way of justifying negative thinking. Go for something great." —Dr. Bob Rotella

45. "Every day may not be good ... but there's something good in every day." — Alice Morse Earle

46. "I do not believe in taking the right decision, I take a decision and make it right." —Muhammad Ali Jinnah

47. "Count your blessings. Focus on what you've got. Spread the positive vibes." — Jyoti Patel

48. "You can often change your circumstances by changing your attitude." —Eleanor Roosevelt

49. "A positive attitude causes a chain reaction of positive thoughts, events, and outcomes. It is a catalyst, and it sparks extraordinary results." —Wade Boggs

50. "It isn't what you have or who you are or where you are or what you are doing that makes you happy or unhappy. It is what you think about it." —Dale Carnegie

51. "No one else makes us angry. We make ourselves angry when we surrender control of our attitude." —Jim Rohn

52. "I hope the millions of people I've touched have the optimism and desire to share their goals and hard work and persevere with a positive attitude." — Michael Jordan

53. "You always pass failure on the way to success." —Mickey Rooney

55. "Our attitude towards life determines life's attitude towards us." —John Mitchell

56. "Everywhere you go, make positive deposits rather than negative withdrawals. You can be a people builder." —Joel Osteen

57. "Optimism is a happiness magnet. If you stay positive, good things and good people will be drawn to you." —Mary Lou Retton

58. "Everyone has his burden. What counts is how you carry it." —Merle Miller

59. "Keep a positive outlook even when faced with life challenges." —Catherine Pulsifer

60. "A truly happy person is one who can enjoy the scenery while on a detour." — Unknown

61. "I don't think of all the misery but of the beauty that still remains." —Anne Frank

62. "Weakness of attitude becomes weakness of character." —<u>Albert Einstein</u>

63. "Always keep that happy attitude. Pretend that you are holding a beautiful fragrant bouquet." —Earl Nightingale

64. "Hard work keeps the wrinkles out of the mind and spirit." —Helena Rubinstein

65. "Perpetual optimism is a force multiplier." —Colin Powell

66. "A positive attitude is not something that you acquire but instead is the active mental process of pointing your thoughts away from despair to that of rejoicing." —Byron R. Pulsifer

67. "Choose the positive. You have choice, you are master of your attitude, choose the positive, the constructive. Optimism is a faith that leads to success." —Bruce Lee

68. "Sometimes it takes a wrong turn to get you to the right place." —Mandy Hale

69. "When you are enthusiastic about what you do, you feel this positive energy. It's very simple." —Paulo Coelho

70. "In one minute you can change your attitude, and, in that minute, you can change your entire day." —Spencer Johnson

71. "Virtually nothing on earth can stop a person with a positive attitude who has his goal clearly in sight." —Denis Waitley

72. "Positive thinking will let you do everything better than negative thinking." —Zig Ziglar

73. "You need an attitude of service. You're not just serving yourself. You help others to grow up and you grow with them." —Oprah Winfrey

74. "All your dreams can come true f you have the courage to pursue them." —Walt Disney

75. "Men do not attract that which they want, but that which they are." —James Allen

#HeWhoPersists #BlackSuperHero #AttitudeDeterminesYourAltitude101 #YouBetNotQuit

Made in the USA
Columbia, SC
05 October 2023